Introduction

In the dark churchyard a strange shadowy figure appears by a tomb. Is it a **ghost**, or just the moon playing tricks?

Thousands of people say they have seen or heard ghosts. Some people say they have seen the ghosts of men and women who have died. Other people say they have seen the ghosts of animals or of objects, such as ships. Some ghosts are said to throw objects, or to start fires.

Some people believe that there are no such things as ghosts. They have spoken to witnesses and studied different types of ghost. **Ghost investigators** try to explain what a ghost is and what it does.

So far nobody has been able to prove that ghosts actually exist. Nobody can explain what ghosts are. However, thousands of people have seen or heard a ghost. Something has happened to these people ... but what could it be?

Where did the ghostly dog come from?

The Tidworth drummer

Poltergeist is the name given to a particular type of haunting. It is a German word which means noisy ghost. Poltergeists often bang on furniture and walls. Objects may move around on their own and fires may break out for no reason.

One of the earliest records of a poltergeist haunting happened in Tidworth, Wiltshire, in 1666. A tramp was annoying people by playing his drum and was sent to prison by a **magistrate**. Soon afterwards strange noises were heard in the magistrate's house. They sounded like a muffled drum being beaten. Local people soon spread stories that a demon drummer was haunting the magistrate as punishment for locking the tramp up.

The local vicar, Joseph Glanvill, investigated the drumming noises. He couldn't find any signs of a trick. After a few weeks the tramp was let out of prison and left the area. Soon afterwards the strange noises stopped.

The Mulhouse poltergeist

In 1980 a poltergeist struck a family home in Mulhouse, France.

The poltergeist trouble began with loud bangs and knocking on doors and windows. Later, strange smells spread through the house. Rooms suddenly got very cold. Objects moved from one place to another through solid barriers. For example, a roll of film moved from inside a camera to behind a picture. Inside the camera was a sheet of paper with a drawing on. The camera had been sealed the whole time.

The drawing found folded inside the sealed camera

For a short time the poltergeist seemed to be angry with the mother, Carla. She was hit by flying objects and badly bruised. Twice when she was in a room the door suddenly slammed shut and locked itself. After several months the poltergeist became quieter. Eventually the poltergeist stopped.

Ghost investigators tried to contact the poltergeist.

The Enfield haunting

The poltergeist of Enfield is one of the most famous poltergeists. It was investigated by scientific researchers. Many newspapers printed stories about it.

The haunting began in August 1977 at the home of the Harper family. Objects moved by themselves. A chest of drawers in the children's bedroom moved several centimetres. Then loud knocking sounds were heard. Mrs Harper called her neighbours in. They also heard the sounds, but they couldn't see what was making them. The police were called. They saw furniture move about and heard the knocking.

This metal teapot rocked back and forth, then the lid bent.

After several days of this, the Harpers phoned a local newspaper. When the press photographer came he was hit on the head by a large toy and got a nasty bruise.

Over the next few weeks the poltergeist became more dramatic. Once one of the children was whirled around as if by invisible hands. Another time her bedclothes were ripped off as she slept.

By February of 1978 the poltergeist became quieter. It stopped completely by November.

Some of the things that the poltergeist broke in the Harper's home

Phantom dancers

Some ghosts are heard but never seen.

Bath is a beautiful city in England. It has many old houses where rich families used to go on holiday. One house, in Edward Street, is now haunted.

From time to time people in the house hear the sounds of stately dance music, heels tapping on wooden floorboards and laughter. The noises come from the front room which was a ballroom in the 18th century. As soon as anyone goes into the room the sounds stop. No ghosts have ever been seen.

Bayham Abbey in Sussex is also haunted by strange sounds. Some visitors to the ruins have heard the sound of monks singing and chanting as if in the distance. The music lasts for a few seconds, then fades away.

Phantom noises

Two phantom ladies haunt **Hampton Court** Palace. They are invisible but very noisy.

In 1829 the tomb of Mrs Penn, foster mother of King Edward VI, was moved. Afterwards the sound of a spinning wheel was heard in an empty ground floor room. It stopped whenever anyone went in. The haunting gradually faded after the tomb was mended and put back.

The second phantom lady is much more disturbing. Her terrible screams have echoed down the gallery outside the chapel. Only a few people have heard these terrifying screams. They sound suddenly and without warning, at any time of the day.

People say that these are the phantom screams of Queen Catherine Howard. She was the fifth wife of Henry VIII. In November 1541 she was staying in Hampton Court when she was arrested in the gallery. She screamed in terror as the soldiers seized her. It is these screams that are still heard from time to time.

“Why don’t they come?”

There is a ghostly old man at Kensington Palace, London. People who live and work there often see him. He looks worried and he sits at a window staring out. He watches a weathercock on the roof and mutters “Why don’t they come?”

Nobody is frightened of him because he doesn’t bother anyone. He usually vanishes after a few seconds.

This is the ghost of King George II. He was the King of Britain from 1727 to 1760.

In October 1760 George was staying at Kensington Palace. He was ill and waiting for some important news by ship from Germany. There was a strong westerly wind so no ships could enter the British harbour. Every day, George stared at the weathercock hoping the wind would change. Sadly, he died before the news arrived. Now his ghost sits waiting for the news.

The Rose Room ghost

In 1938 the Queen of the Netherlands visited the United States of America. She stayed at the **White House** in Washington where the American President lives. One evening, the Queen heard a knock at her bedroom door.

The Queen of the Netherlands

When she opened it she saw the ghost of President Abraham Lincoln who had died in 1865. The Queen fainted in horror.

The bedroom the Queen stayed in is called the Rose Room. Many people have claimed to have seen President Lincoln in this room.

These presidents have seen the ghost of Abraham Lincoln.

Eisenhower

Roosevelt

The Roman legion

In 1953 a plumber called Harry Martindale was working in the cellar of an old house in York.

Suddenly he heard two trumpet blasts, and saw a man on a horse come out of the wall. Then came more men on foot. They were wearing kilt-like skirts and carrying spears. The didn't seem to be walking on the floor because their knees were at ground level.

The men looked very depressed as they walked past Harry and vanished through another wall.

Harry ran upstairs to tell his work mates. They didn't believe him but the owner of the house did. He had often heard strange noises in the cellar.

Hundreds of years ago a unit of Roman infantry had been stationed in York. Like the ghosts they wore kilt-like skirts and carried spears. When the cellar floor was dug up, the remains of a Roman road were found several centimetres below the floor. The ghosts had been marching along this road which was why Harry could not see below their knees.

The cellar where Harry Martindale saw the Roman soldiers.

The battle of ghosts

During the English Civil War in 1643 a group of farm workers were walking in the fields in Warwickshire. Suddenly a group of mounted soldiers galloped past. Next came several thousand soldiers on foot. The workers watched as the soldiers fought to the death. Then the soldiers vanished into thin air.

The story of the phantom army spread quickly. More phantom armies were seen over the following weeks. King Charles heard about the ghosts and sent a team of army officers to investigate. The officers spoke to several witnesses and even saw the ghosts themselves.

They said that the ghosts were re-enacting the events of the battle. Among the ghosts the officers recognized several friends who had been killed. But they also recognized men who were still alive such as Prince Rupert, the famous cavalry commander.

Prince Rupert in battle

The ghostly gunfighters

In 1876 the famous gambler and **gunfighter** Wild Bill Hickok was playing cards in a **saloon** in Deadwood, South Dakota. Suddenly the door of the saloon flew open. A drunken cowboy walked in, pulled out a gun and shot Hickok in the back. Hickok died instantly and was buried in the local cemetery. His ghost was seen near his grave several times.

Billy the Kid first murdered a man in a fight when he was 12. Later he robbed banks, stole horses and killed at least 21 men. In 1881 he was in Fort Sumner, New Mexico where he came face to face with **Sheriff** Pat Garrett. Garrett pulled out his gun and shot him dead. Since then Billy the Kid's ghost has been seen several times in Fort Sumner.

The ghostly hitch-hiker

In 1978 a South African policeman saw a ghost. He was patrolling a lonely area on his motorbike when he saw a young woman standing by the roadside. She had her thumb out for a ride. He stopped for her. He said he was going back to Uniondale and asked her if she would like a lift there. The girl nodded.

He set off with her and speeded up to 50 kilometres per hour for about five minutes. Suddenly his motorbike swerved. He turned round to see if the girl was safe. She had vanished. He looked around to see if the girl had fallen off. She was nowhere to be seen. He carefully rode back over his route. There was no sign of the girl anywhere.

The policeman went on with his patrol. When he got back to the police station, he told them what had happened. The station chief told him that the same thing had happened to a motorist a few weeks earlier. In the following weeks, there were two more stories about the young woman who hitched a ride and then suddenly vanished.

Maria Roux died in a car crash where the ghostly hitch-hiker was seen. Was she the ghost trying to hitch a ride?

Mount St Helens erupting

In April 1980 a motorist in Washington State picked up an old woman who was hitch-hiking. The old woman said that the man should get out of the area. She said the nearby Mount St Helens was about to explode. Several other motorists also gave the strange old woman a lift. She gave them all the same warning. On 8 May Mount St Helens blew itself apart in a massive volcanic eruption.

The phantom Admiral

On 22 June 1893 Lady Tryon held a dinner party for a few friends in London. Her husband, **Admiral** Sir George Tryon, was at sea with his fleet. Lady Tryon showed her guests into the dining room, then left to check the dinner.

A few minutes later the guests were surprised to see Admiral Tryon. He walked down the stairs and came into the dining room. Some of his friends spoke to him, but he ignored them. Then he walked away. When Lady Tryon came back, her guests told her what had happened. She said her husband was at sea. But the guests were sure they had seen the Admiral.

Some days later news came that Admiral Tryon's ship had sunk and he was dead. He had died a few hours before he had been seen by his wife's guests. Perhaps he had wanted to take a last look at his home.

The Flying Dutchman

Many people have seen a ghostly ship while at sea. In 1899 the steamship Hannah Regan was at sea off the cost of China. Its Captain saw a strange-looking ship. It was very old with an old-fashioned rig. It moved as if it were in a storm, and had wind-torn sails. It stayed in sight for about 20 minutes and was seen by a lot of sailors. Then it faded to a shadow and vanished.

This German Captain saw The Flying Dutchman during World War 2.

During World War II a German **U-boat** crew saw the same ghostly ship. They were so frightened of it that they would rather go into enemy waters than stay where they were. Both the Captain of the Hannah Regan and the German crew had seen **the Flying Dutchman**.

This was a Dutch ship that had sailed into a bad storm many years ago. The crew begged the Captain to pray to God to save them. But he was angry, and cursed God. Instead he asked for the devil to help him. The devil came at once and promised to save the ship. In return for the favour, the Captain was doomed to sail for ever on the ship, bringing bad luck to all who saw him.

The Wild Hunt

There are many legends about **the Wild Hunt.** One famous story from Cornwall is about a farmer who was walking home late at night. He saw a pack of black hounds led by a huntsman dressed in black. The huntsman blew his horn and they all stopped. The

huntsman threw a bundle at the farmer, then quickly disappeared. The farmer bent down to open the bundle. Inside was the dead body of his son.

Stories about the Wild Hunt are usually very frightening. The Dark Huntsman brings death and destruction with him. In some cases the black dogs are seen alone during the daytime.

What are ghosts?

Some people do not believe in ghosts. They think that these strange happenings are caused by natural events. Bright lights can cast strange shadows. Other people believe that ghosts do exist. Here are some explanations of the strange activities.

GHOSTLY PEOPLE

The most common ghosts are of people who once lived. There are two different types of ghostly people.

Classic ghosts

The first type appears after the person has died. Usually the ghost repeats the same movement. The ghost of King George II watching the weathercock is of this type. This type is known as a **classic ghost**.

Crisis ghosts

Some ghostly people appear only once. These ghosts appear at the moment a person dies. The ghost of Admiral Tryon was of this type. They are known as **crisis ghosts**.

Explanations

Some people believe that ghosts of people who are dead are recordings of past events. They think that houses can record events just like a video recorder can record television programmes. The recording can then be replayed. When this happens, people see a ghost. When the recording has worn out, the ghosts stop appearing. Many ghosts do stop appearing after a time.

Like the Roman soldiers in York, the dancers at Bath might be a recording of past events.

The ghostly Roman soldiers seen in York may be of this type. The man who saw the ghosts said they ignored him as they marched past. The witness had also said the ghosts appeared to be very upset and depressed. Perhaps the emotions of the soldiers caused the recording.

Crisis ghosts may also be caused by strong emotions. A dying person may want to visit home or talk to a friend. It may be that this strong emotion can send a picture to the place or person. This image would appear as a ghost. Admiral Tryon knew that he would die as his ship sank. He had not seen his home for many weeks. Perhaps he somehow projected his ghost to appear in the place he loved.

NON-HUMAN GHOSTS

Supernatural creatures

The Dark Huntsman and his dogs are not ghosts of dogs and a hunter that actually lived. They are supernatural creatures.

Explanation

Some people think stories of the Wild Hunt are left over from the old pagan religion. These ghosts appear only in areas where there were pagan stories of a god named **Odin**. Odin was said to ride at night to search for the souls of dying warriors. The Wild Hunt is said to ride at night to find souls of the dead.

Poltergeists

Poltergeists move objects around and cause strange noises. People who have investigated poltergeists have noticed that the haunting seems to be focused on one person. The poltergeist is only active if this person is present. The 'focus person' is usually young, female and under stress of some kind.

Explanation

Some people think that the focus person is somehow creating the poltergeist. The young person may be using some kind of mental energy without realizing it. Nobody knows quite how this could happen. Other investigators think the focus person is faking the events to draw attention to her problems.

This girl was troubled by a poltergeist.

Investigating ghosts

There are people who investigate ghosts for their job. They usually have qualifications in the sciences.

Ghost investigators go to places where many people have seen ghosts. They use special equipment to investigate ghosts.

Cameras are set up to take a photograph of anything which moves. Tape recorders are set to start recording if there is a noise. People often say that a room gets colder when a ghost appears. Special thermometers are used to take the temperature of a room over several hours. The investigators make sure that no one can play a trick.

Tape recorders will pick up strange sounds.

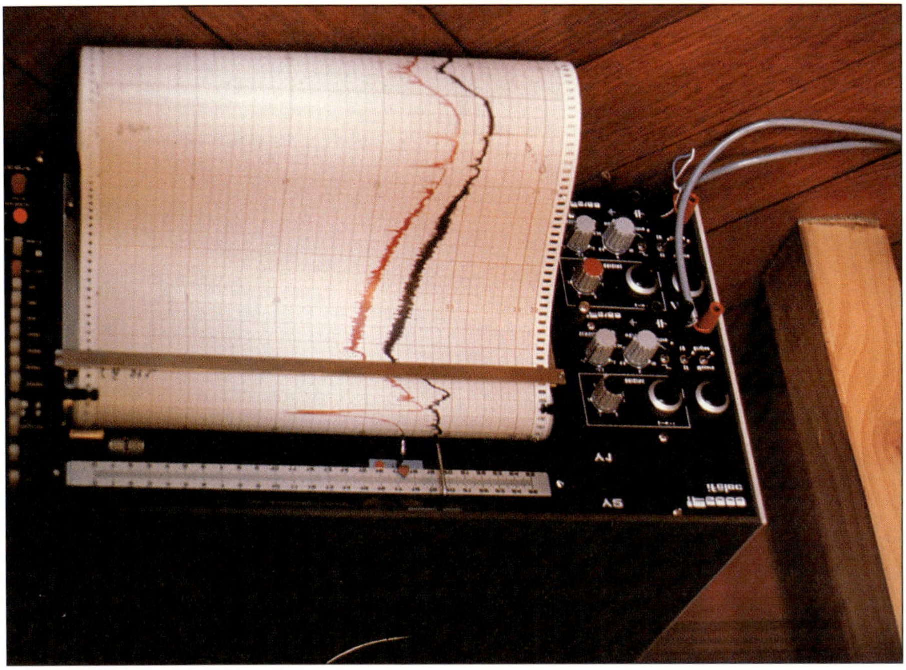

Temperature readings show changes when ghosts appear.

Seals are placed on doors and windows to show if they are opened. Fine flour is sprinkled on the floor to record any footprints.

The ghost investigators will then write about what they find. The stories might be published in a magazine about ghosts.

Most ghost investigators are members of the Society for Psychical Research. This Society gathers stories of ghosts from all around Britain. It publishes stories of ghosts and investigations in a regular magazine.

Glossary

admiral A senior officer in the navy. Admirals usually command a fleet of several ships.

classic ghost A ghost of a dead person which repeats the same action over and over again.

crisis ghost A ghost which is seen only once, usually when a person dies.

Flying Dutchman, The A ghostly ship seen by many people, usually in the Indian or Pacific Oceans.

ghost A phantom figure which can appear and vanish. Ghosts may be of people, animals or objects.

ghost investigator A person who uses scientific instruments to discover more facts about ghosts.

gunfighter A cowboy or lawman in the American West who could shoot accurately with his pistol.

Hampton Court A palace south west of London, England. It was built in the 16th century.

hitch-hiker A person who asks strangers for a lift in a car or on a motorbike.

legion A group of infantry soldiers in the ancient Roman Empire.

magistrate A type of judge who deals with small crimes.

Odin A pagan god once worshipped in Germany, England and Scandinavia. Odin was a god of warriors and the sky.

phantom Another word for a ghost.

poltergeist A type of ghost that moves objects and causes loud noises. The word is German for noisy ghost.

saloon A bar or restaurant in the American West.

sheriff A type of lawman in the American West, usually in charge of keeping the law in a small town.

U-boat A German submarine used to sink enemy ships during wartime.

White House, The A large house in the city of Washington, USA. It is the home to the President of the USA.

Wild Hunt, The A terrifying haunting of dogs and a huntsman who seeks the souls of the dead.

Index

steam train

holiday poster

At the hotel

On Tuesday Edward and Victoria had dinner at their hotel. A maid gave them their food.

maids

hotel

On the beach

On Wednesday Edward went for a ride on a donkey. Victoria made a sandcastle with her bucket and spade.

A Victorian Seaside Holiday

Contents

A seaside holiday

On Monday Edward and Victoria went on holiday to the seaside. They went on a steam train.

buckets and spades

donkey
ride

In the sea

On Thursday Edward and Victoria put on their bathing costumes. They went in the sea.

bathing machines

bathing costumes

On the promenade

On Friday Edward and Victoria went to see the Punch and Judy Show. Then they had an ice cream.

ice cream seller

Punch and Judy puppets

On the pier

On Saturday Edward and Victoria went on a merry-go-round. Then they went to see a show at the theatre.

merry-go-round

theatre poster

At the shops

At the end of the holiday Edward and Victoria went to the shops. They got postcards and sticks of rock to take home.

postcard

rock poster

Index